WHIMSICAL HEIGHTS

A SHORT POETRY COLLECTION

DANIELLE BERNAE WRIGHT

Copyright © 2024 by Danielle Bernae Wright. All rights reserved. No part of this book may be reproduced or used in any manner without written permission of the copyright owner.

Dedication

I dedicate this poetry book to all my fellow Hot Air Balloon Pilots who have channeled their pain and struggles and used it as fuel to reach new heights. Please don't stop soaring and exploring beyond your horizon.

Table of Contents

Hot Air Balloon	1
Mental Health	**2**
Tired	2
Guilt Be Like	5
Trauma and Ego	6
Of Psyche and Senses	7
Deep Breaths	8
Depression Be Like	9
Drunkenness: Dejection or Delight?	10
Domestic Violence	11
Every Day Life In The Big Apple	**12**
Strangers on a Train	13
Wash and Repeat	14
January Cold	15
Walking on Whispers of Flames and Frost	16
Dear Neighbor	18
Don't Take Life for Granted	19
Love And Longing	**20**

David: Open Questions to Unrequited Love	21
A Cosmic Boom	23
The Alpha, The Omega, The Dream of Us	24
Single Woes for Single Hoes	25
Orbit	26
Pals	27
Love Letters To Self	**28**
Danielle	29
Pineapples or Acorns?	30
I am	31
Theft of Identity	32

Hot Air Balloon

We ascend into the hot air balloon
A craft lighter than air
I am with my new beau
I am in love with my beau
I am in love with nature
I am in love with the sky
I am enveloped in magic
I look up at the enormous sight
It is vibrant with rich colors of azul and zest
So lovely, I can't catch my breath
We climb higher and higher into the heavens on an enchanting climb
Suspended above earth on the whispers of a poet's rhyme
Silhouetted against the afternoon sky
We litter the heavens like butterflies
And just like any other dream that ended too soon
We returned to the Earth in our hot air balloon

MENTAL HEALTH

Tired

I am tired
Mentally tired
Physically tired
Spiritually tired
This is a new year
But no new me
Just a tired me
Tired of people: selfish-type people
Draining-type people, negative-type people
I am tired of the media:
social media, news media, all the media
that keeps telling me to stay woke
I am so woke, I am insomniac
My mental wellness has been hijacked
I am tired
Tired of the War on Christmas
The war on Easter, the war on Religion, the
war in the Middle East
I am tired of the war on Pancakes and Everything Bread
I am tired of having to explain myself
I am tired of failing to reclaim myself
I am tired of long workdays and short weekends, and
I am short on patience
I do my best to be kind, to be considerate, so that I am not a
hypocrite
I step slowly toward positivity with heavy sighs

I want change! I need change
But what type of change will help?
Is it a me-type change? Or they-type change?
Or we-type change?
I don't know what will help
To make me feel less tired of the world

Guilt Be Like

It seems that my past will always be with me
Side by side
My shadow in the sun
Forever reminding me of all the pain I've endured
And all the wrong I have done
The dark thoughts comfort me
Blanketing me with doubt and ugliness
It weighs me down with shame
It robs me of happiness
Because I can't get past it
I can't get over or though it
These dark thoughts welcome pain
For pain is what I deserve
It is what I have earned
It is what I have allowed for myself
I don't know how to live in the light of joy
I always revert to the feelings of inadequacy
Reeling in self-inflicted pain
In the still of a darkness, I become a shadow

Trauma and Ego

Deep inside me, there is a broken girl
who sits in the corner of my psyche
She has experienced much pain and much sadness
I want to hug her and tell *her* everything will be okay
That *Her* feelings matter
That *She* is not forgotten
I want to cry with *her*, but I don't!
I ignore *her*
If I give *her* a voice, *she* might say something to
destroy all **we** have built
I am too busy living from my corner of the psyche
I have been given a platform and a loud voice
She sits quietly and motionless in her corner
She is ever-present and forever watching me
She longs for my company
On nights when my guard is down from drinking
too many libations
I cozy up to *her*
I like how *she* keeps me company on those
eccentric nights

Of Psyche and Senses

I am living between two worlds
Two times, two different chapters of my life
I am in the present re-living my past
A smell, a sight, a sound
Transports me back to a memory
I experience this on-and-off all day
Seems like every day lately
I can see a person in the likeness of a person that I once knew
All those feelings start to flow through me
I am suffering memories I forgot
Memories I lost
One scent, one sight, one sound, one likeness
And I am back in that moment
It is crazy how the brain works
How the brain copes
I wonder who is in control?
On this passage of psyche and senses

Deep Breaths

Take a deep breath
Now, take another
You are okay
I am okay
We live in a crazy world
Where we hear of wars in faraway countries
And political wars at home
We are divided on difference of opinions
Even though we all desire the same things
Freedom to live, love, and thrive
How did society become so insensitive to other people's views?
Because they don't share the same religion, social background, or hue?
The threats of death and poverty are consuming
All gloom all doom all the time
It's suffocating
Debilitating
I take a deep breath
It calms me in these crazy times

Depression Be Like

I have stumbled and fallen into a dark place
Similar to a hole but less depressing
It is quiet here and I am not in any danger
I am comfortable but I don't care to stay long
But I don't care to leave anytime soon
I am not hurt in a physical way, but I have chronic emotional injury
It is causing a dull ache to my happiness
When I am down in this allegorical hole
I am protected from the weight of the world's nonsense
In here, I find it easier to fake smile through meaningless interaction
Which is pretty much all of them

Drunkenness: Dejection or Delight?

My therapist says alcohol is a depressant,
but I don't feel depressed
I feel alive, I feel significant
Even confident
So, when I hang out with friends
3-4-6 glasses of wine makes sense
My drinking is not a problem
I can afford it
Wine is cheap and it's only an Uber home
I can handle myself
I never sleep alone
Now, I admit that work suffers
It's nothing coffee can't fix
A *"promise to do better"* can't correct
And the missed deadlines managers have come to expect
The loud sounds of the bar with the florescent lights
Blur the lines of what is right
I drink more and more to numb the pain
All my real and imagined problems wash away
I don't want to stop
I don't want to give it up
I don't want it to take all I am worth
I'll consider things more after one more glass
Will there be any concessions reached in this
drunk impasse?

Domestic Violence

My life is a wreck
I cry uncontrollable
As he strengthens his grip around my neck
This has become my new normal
The honeymoon phase ended when summer ended
My partner's cold treatment toward me
Began just as the snow blanketed December Mornings
And now I mourn
A life that should have been
There was no substance abuse
No work or financial strain
None of the usual culprits to blame
No impactful event to cause a shift
No lynchpin to the decline of our partnership
In the beginning and over time
there were signs
yellow flags, orange flags and red flags
burning bright in the colors of fire
I was a moth drawn to the heat of the flame
I was a woman drawn to the idea of a new last name
Is this to be my life?
Or my death?

EVERY DAY LIFE IN THE BIG APPLE

Strangers on a Train

I had my ear pods in with The Chainsmokers turned up
I was on the C train headed home to Harlem
An odd-looking woman boarded the train
I couldn't help but make eye contact with her
We held it for a minute
I felt I could see right through her, right to myself
The lady was sipping on a red slushy
I watched as she simultaneously changed her socks and dug into her purse for cigarettes
As her cigarette dangled from her mouth, she looked at me
"Does this train go to Penn Station?"
"Yes," I responded
I watched her and I was intrigued by her
She seemed mentally fractured
But her spirit was expansive
I could tell
She and I continued communicating, without words
Only long incessant stares from across the train
When we pulled into Penn Station
She walked off but not before she said goodbye
I said, "Be safe out there"

Wash and Repeat

With all the loud clatter of a WAR-ing life
People are unable to hear your point of view
They can begin to hear your truth when you are
down in the trenches with them
It is only then that you can speak to them about
how to find peace and safety

January Cold

It was January and the frigid temps had finally arrived
I don't know why I was outside with summer crocs and socks
Old Man Winter was finally awake from his nap
And with gusto, the wing gusted
Pipes busted
The train vents lusted...
At the frozen puddles of water and pee on the streets
And the night frost nipped, nipped, nipped
Relentlessly at all my tips
Nose tip, fingertips, toe tips
Of course! I was outside with a flimsy hat on
Not worth the three dollars that I paid five for
I walked the dog, in a hurry, in a fury
How was the dog not cold?
I guess the built-in fur jacket helps
I walked fast to shelter from the old man's wintery laugh
Howling the leaves to dance in cadence and commanding my nose to tears?

Walking on Whispers
of Flames and Frost

I rise to the most beautiful morning of a distant land, feeling a little distanced from self
The thin linen blankets hug me, beg me to stay in bed a little longer
I keep the sheets entertained with my tossing and turning, as I run along the edges of my vivid dreams
The room is furnished with local art wrapped in dark wood and colorful wallpaper
It is an outward expression of my inner self
The room has a distinct smell of lemon notes with a hint of salt
It is a fragrant expression of my spiritual self
For lemons brighten and salt enhances
I witness the waves dancing the waltz with their lifelong partner, the shoreline
In a continuous embrace, they bop and breeze back and forth to the melody of nature and love
Standing on the balcony, I watch the performance of the ocean, in awe of its beauty
The sun watches me, in awe of my beauty
The sun and I are almost one and the same
Both voyeurs, looking and sitting bright in our fullness
I am full of life, full of love, full of excitement
I sip from a glass overflowing with abundance
I am full of shine and fire like the sun

I am full of depth and reflection like the ocean
I love the way life presses its joy into my being until I am whole
I enjoy soaking up the beautiful nature of a distant land
And then, I wake up! A twist unseen, for my dreams took a spin
I sat with my husband, waited for his chemo session to begin
I had dozed off to escape the cold
The cold feelings of the hospital, the cold feelings of uncertainty, denial, rage
The weight of my eyelids helps me to disengage
I sat in the hard chair, falling asleep with my head in my hands
Allowing my mind to wander into imaginative lands
As my husband undergoes treatment, I undergo magic and I travel
To the beach or any place out of reach
It's how I cope, so I don't scream
I am comforted as I daydream

Dear Neighbor

We have been passing each other for months
But today was the first time I saw you
Truly saw you
Your pain was cleverly hidden behind your beautiful smile
I was attracted to the pain
A longing for connection
That aches with its hands reaching out
Into the shadows of a familiar happiness
I sit on your couch observing you as you move around
Talking about everything EXCEPT for the one thing
Your Explosion
A bomb of a million splinters into your heart
Dividing you in two, three, maybe four pieces of self
Tonight, I drink rum with one of those versions of you
You fascinate me with your life experiences
You have a golden heart and eyes warm and brown like pretzels
You have shown me a kindness that I will hold
In my heart forever
You get me and that is something I have never *gotten* before
I pray to God for His favor upon you
I am happy to meet you

Don't Take Life for Granted

Oh! What a joy I experienced
I came to awareness from a deep slumber and was
in sync with my life force
I had left the window open
My sense of hearing was the first to be awakened.
The whirl of city noise
The garbage truck, the fire truck, the rustling of trees and
non-distinct chatter
My sense of smell was the next
Dried lavender by my bedside
Finally, my sense of sight
I open my eyes to the weak glow of sunlight coming though
the sheer curtain.
Oh, what a joy it is to be alive

LOVE AND LONGING

David: Open Questions to Unrequited Love

What color are your eyes?
A tincture of admiration
To watch me with kindness, curiosity, and delight.
What does your voice sound like?
Grounding every conversation
Every whisper in my ear
I know it sounds sweet
Every time you say my name
Do you smell good?
I lean into you and kiss your collar
Kiss your cheek and inhale your being
Is your hug strong?
Please use it to embrace me, comfort me, and secure me in your world
Are your hands soft?
Imagine how they twine into mine
While we walk the busy streets of the city
And the quiet paths of nature
How tall are you?
I want to look up to you with love and respect
Balancing on my toes with my arms around your neck
What do your kisses taste like?
Are your lips sweet?
Is your hair soft?

I want to run my fingers through it
While you drink from the well between my thighs,
Quenching your thirst
Are you strong?
I want to feel the weight of you on top of me
channeling deep into my womb
Deep into my universe
Can I trust you?
Is it safe to love you?
Is it safe to submit to you?
I want the opportunity to know you
Truly and deeply, intimately, and entirely
Good, bad, and in-between
I want to give you the same opportunity

A Cosmic Boom

Take my hand and walk with me
Get lost in me
Fall into my presence
Every encounter is a present
A gift of moments
Which build and connect
One person to the next
Hold on to me
Long and tight
Till my senses ignite
Kiss me deeply
Let me get lost in the scent of you
Until it makes no sense
That I am still holding onto you
Use your eyes to capture every pixel of my beauty
Etch those images into the corners of your heart
So that when we part
My essence will remain with you, until the next
time that I can be with you

The Alpha, The Omega, The Dream of Us

I love you
From my past life
Into this life
To the next life too
I love you for as far back as I existed
To as far a future that I will exist
Our encounter was brief
But not random
Your energy was a familiar phantom
Your smile lit a chord in my soul
Just like that, my universe was whole
I have seen your smile before
I have experienced your love in all my lives
and the taste of you, I will spend infinity longing to savor

Single Woes for Single Hoes

I was in a long-term relationship
And then I was long-term single
Cause I kept having short-term connections
With people who had short-term intentions
And short-term commitments
I was committed
To being all the way honest
True transparency
But that didn't work out well
So I used lies and half-truths
And attracted half-ass men
All the way grown but halfway youths
I am stuck in a culture where swiping is easy
But dating is hard…
Even harder to sit on the sidelines
But it is easy to get in the game and get caught-up
But not caught long-term

Orbit

Oh soulmate, eternal lover, forever beau
Where art thou?
I am sitting by the water, propped beside a tree
Wishing you were here with me
I am watching the boats
I am enjoying this record-hot summer day in the shade
It's beautiful out here
I plan to wait for you until the stars light the sky
And the earth illuminates from the glow of fireflies
I will wait all night if I must
I'll wait until the sun lifts the world in lightness
And the sky is effervescent blue
I will be here and waiting for you

Pals

He puts the pal in platonic
We are on the path to a solid friendship
Then one night his hug causes a shift
And I have a firestorm of lust-filled what-ifs
Most nights, I smoke weed with him on the balcony
And go home to masturbate at the thought of him inside of me
I'm dancing to a tune of moral hypocrisy
And for the sake of my *saint-ness*
I minimize and rationalize all the lies
Stuck between what is right and what I desire
Too bad he is attracted to women who are white and petite
Opposite of me
I'm thick and sweet, and deep
Warm like tea
And choosy
Like moms who choose Jif
I choose the friendship
Not only to avoid a rift
But because our bond has been a gift

LOVE LETTERS TO SELF

Danielle

I walk hard
I laugh loud
I have an opinion about everything and always
My head is constantly filled with abstract ideas
And my heart with love and temper
I am certain my way is the right one
I sleep wild
I don't know the lyrics to most songs
And I can't sing or dance, but I still sing and dance
I am shy but outspoken
I apologize for none of this because all of this is who I am

Pineapples or Acorns?

Living in a world where everyone is the same and I am different feels painful
I used to think everyone couldn't be wrong
Singing the same songs
Of ego, hatred of self, and others
I am different and I see that now clearly
I feel lonely
Even in a room full of humans, I feel extraterrestrial
A being from outer space
Another time, another place
I spend too much time on the offensive
Proving my intentions are pure
I spend too much time on the defensive
Protecting my kindness that is often mistaken for weakness
Am I an Acorn in a Fruit Salad?
Or a Pineapple pregnant on an oak tree?
Futile with growth?
Or stunted in misunderstanding

I am

I am a woman
A beautiful black celestial being of a woman
I am a sister, aunt, niece, cousin
I receive and give love freely
I am a poet
I put thoughts to paper to help make sense of human experience
I am strong and fit
I do repetitions and sets to build mental, physical, and emotional endurance
I am a veteran
I served my country
I salute all those who sacrificed before me and all who will come next
I am a social worker
I am here to help you download and decode the drama
I champion so many roles
Lit ablaze by the fire inside of me
Made greater by all those who love and support me
Thank you!

Theft of Identity

How could I be mad at you?
For having low self-esteem, low confidence, no respect for yourself
So much that you continuously copy small pieces from me
so that you feel complete
Thankfully for me
I am so grounded in who I am
Where I am going
Where I have been
that no amount of pieces you copy from
me will take from me
You could never be me
You would probably argue against what I am saying
But look at yourself
Are you not an imitation of me
Wanting to be like me
In the way I light this life ablaze
With zest and curiosity
Never mediocrity
I rap, you rap
Just like that
I march on in
Colorful as sin
From a front row seat
You see me
And you are compelled to be like me

Loud and free
Suddenly, you are into all of the things I am into
All the things that represent me
It feels like a theft of my identify
I have never witnessed your expression or desire
To having liked any of the things I admire
Your feelings were once sharp with criticism
Now they trace mine like a quiet plagiarism

Dear Readers,

I want to take a moment to express my heartfelt gratitude to each of you. Thank you for taking the time to read my work and for allowing my words to resonate with you. Your support, encouragement, and feedback mean the world to me.

Writing is a journey and knowing that my words have reached and touched others makes it even more meaningful. I hope my poetry continues to inspire, comfort, and connect with you.

Thank you for being a part of this journey with me.

With love and gratitude,

Danielle Bernae Wright

www.ingramcontent.com/pod-product-compliance
Lightning Source LLC
Chambersburg PA
CBHW031507040426
42444CB00007B/1243